NA

I KISSED A FROG AND
MY PRINCE FORGAVE ME

A Poetic Journey Through Infidelity

PublishAmerica
Baltimore

ISBN: 1-4241-0027-5
PUBLISHED BY PUBLISHAMERICA, LLLP
www.publishamerica.com
Baltimore

Printed in the United States of America

This book is dedicated to my husband and to our marriage. In losing us we found each other again. You will always be my Prince . I love you!

Acknowledgements:

The biggest and most important thank you goes to my husband. Without his strength and support in my writing this book would not be possible. This is a sensitive subject for us and sharing our ordeal is a big step in healing. I love you Honey!

Many, Many thanks to my friends; Gwen, Marsha, Christy, SC and Deb.

Your ears must be burning from endless conversation! The insights and support have been amazing as well as encouraging. May you always have peace, love and contentment in your lives.

Thank you for helping me heal.

Special thanks to Brenda my therapist who is one of the first people to read my poetry. Thank you Brenda. You helped me see that I'm not the ripple or the stone, but the woman coming out of the wave with her heart in one hand and a sword in the other(you know how scary that is?)

Foreword: Author's Note

Any names or identifying factors (The events are real) in this book have been changed to protect the innocent and not so innocent.

The poems are based on how I felt at the time of writing them and may or may not reflect how I feel today. They were written as a vent, as a tribute, as an awareness, as insight, as an apology, and some just to help tell the story.

The healing process has many stages…For example: confusion, denial, grief, loss, pain,anger,fear, acceptance, and love. I experienced all of them and more. I believe I have come out stronger and clearer for it. I do know I have a greater understanding of myself and my actions. I gain more insight everyday.

The emotional fog does not lift over night. Or even over a fortnight. It clears with layers of reality. At times I just needed a good reality check.

The other person in my life provided that clarity through his words and actions.

The compassion of my husband helped me see how things really were and work through them. We are healing through complete honesty and constant communication. It isn't easy for either of us. I truly am in awe of him. I'm proud of us.

Poetry is about perception. Many poems can stand alone on daily life and not be associated with infidelity. But in this book as a whole they are.

Readers may relate to them differently.

This book was written for the wayward hearts, but I hope others can use it to gain their own understanding. Infidelity happens. It can usually be avoided with awareness and communication.

A wayward heart is human. It loves and loses. It hurts and heals. It loves and triumphs.

We can own and define our mistakes without letting them own and define us.

Thank you for sharing my journey.
Naomi Jo Rush

I KISSED A FROG AND

MY PRINCE

FORGAVE ME

A Poetic Journey Through Infidelity

The Prelude:

"Women can fake orgasms. Men can fake whole relationships"
—Sharon Stone

Double Edged Sword

You should have killed me like you threatened
for I yield a double edged sword.
By putting pen to paper. Telling our story in my word.
In exposing us, I'm hurting others. People are so
judgmental and cruel.
But I learned my family is very strong. They are ready for a duel.
So this is how its going to be. You can try to hide.
In admitting us I own my mistakes. Helping others,
I regain my pride.
Starting out with coffee, you putting yourself in my view.
A plan of pursual. I have learned. I wish I never knew.
I was drawn to you. So I complied, when you asked me
to your store.
I was in a weird place in my life and I sensed you wanted more.
I wouldn't be around for coffee that summer. I wanted
to say goodbye.
You said "Take a drive with me." No pretenses. I knew why.
We ended up in a place that soon came to be our spot.
A summer of secrets and stolen kisses, things got pretty hot.
We clicked so well its hard to explain. Given how different
we are.

Soon we claimed to love each other. Our heads up in the stars.
Hours of talking on the phone, Of secretly seeing each other.
Your wife eventually got suspicious. You felt like you
  would smother.
Yet, when I tried to let you go. You wouldn't let me be.
I figured your love for me was true, since you refused to
  set me free.
On one of your days of drinking, you called me at a horseshow.
Your wife hit redial on the phone. Shit hit the fan
  as you well know.
She found out who I was, and my husband covered up our lie.
He trusted me explicitly, she did not, and we continued to deny.
Never backing off, still going strong, things continued into Fall.
You watching me across the soccer field. I showed up at football.
Then winter came and the Holidays. We both started to stress.
I started in with questions, about our future, and you felt distress.
You said that you were obligated, to work things out with your wife.
I said then please let me go, I'm in too deep, I can't live this double life.
You didn't want to end us, but you wanted to slow down.
I became confused at the change in us, til you kissed me
  in the middle of town.
You were sending me mixed messages. That's when we started
  to fight.
We said some awful things that day. The New Year started
  that night.
We spent a couple weeks barely talking, til one day we made out.
Back together, I asked if I was worth the risk. You said without
  a doubt.
Another month of loving, until your wife got a call about our fun.
That particular rumor wasn't true. But the gossip played with
  a loaded gun.
I heard the strain in your voice. You knew for sure she
  was leaving.
I realized how much you wanted her. It was myself I
  was deceiving.

You'd been telling her she was crazy, and that was just plain wrong.
So I told her we were just friends. And I told her for how long.
That we only talked for hours, never loved, never touched.
I told her you were my best friend and I would miss you
very much.
She insisted we never talk again and that my husband
has to know.
I went home and told him. He took it as quite a blow.
Then your friends, the good ole boys, attempted to step in.
Telling me not to rock the boat. They didn't want their
own wives looking within.
When I found out you were covering your ass, trying to
sell me out.
I told my husband that you claimed to love me. That secret
came about.
Time went by and you ignored me. I was so lost and confused.
My worried husband tried to help me. Just a shell. I felt so used.
Then one day I called you. I wanted some answers. I had to know.
You said that it was all nothing. That I didn't know you. That was
the final blow.
You thought that I was so vulnerable. You forgot about
my strengths.
You pissed me off and that's not smart. I went to greater lengths.
I went home and told my husband we were not just platonic
friends.
The next morning called your wife to meet, but that's not
where this story ends.
I bared my heart and told them everything and yet you continued
to deny.
Your wife said you wanted to kill me. I'm a threat, so I
can understand why.
But I don't hate you. I hate what we did. My caring for you
was real.
I envy you in a way, that you were just pretending, it's easier
for you to deal.

I found out how lucky I am. Something good came from this affair.
Our marriage is stronger than ever. We started a new life to share.
I started this book of poetry. To tell this story in my word.
I know, when it comes out, it will be a double edged sword.

Desparate Thoughts:

"Behind each human face is a hidden world that no one can see. We cannot continue to seek outside ourselves for the things we need from within."

INTO THE LIGHT

Lonely in a full house.
New walls everywhere
Closing in.
Doors locked from the inside
yet there is no escape.
In the darkness,
quiet desperation.
Calling out to empty ears.
Reaching for shadows.
Save me.
Validate my feelings.
Show me this isn't all there is.
I've lost myself to the nothing.
A light shines at the end
of a desolate hall.
Drawn to it like a moth.
A window to the outside world.
So bright and hopeful.
I press my face to warmth
Soaking it all in
On the inside looking out.
Show me the way.
Without breaking the glass
to be free.

HELLO DEAR

Hello Dear.
Can you see me?
My hair has a new style.
I bought a dress in a smaller size.
Put on my best smile.
If I want to hear a compliment.
I will have to wait a while.

Hello Dear,
Can you hear me?
I asked "How was your day?"
You're focused on the TV again.
Do you care what I have to say?
It must be to much to ask
that we talk some more today.

Hello Dear,
Can you feel me?
I'm eager for your touch.
I tried to hug you earlier.
A kiss would mean so much.
It must be hard to take the time.
I'll wait till there's no rush.

Hello Dear,
Do you miss me?
You've been out quite a while.
Wouldn't it be nice to take me dancing?
Show off my great smile?
I hate to be alone all the time
Going that extra mile.

Hello Dear,
If I can't be seen.
I have no value in your eye.
If I can't be heard
I have no reason to cry.
If you can't feel my touch.
Then I no longer care to try.
If you don't miss me.
Then you'll understand
Good-bye.

PEDESTAL

On a pedestal
Like a porcelain doll.
Painted smile, glassy eyes.
Safely on display.
Keeping me from being human.
Void of feelings or dreams.
Without wants or needs.
Easy to keep. Sitting so high-
the sun glared behind me.
You couldn't see, I was breaking.
My smile fading.
Eyes glassed from tears.
On my lonely perch.
Ready for escape.
I closed my eyes.
In a leap of faith...I was falling.
Spiraling downward.
Floating free.
In selfish abandon.
Breathless with awe.
Anticipating my landing;
I open my eyes.
Seeing the hard reality.
I braced myself,
For the inevitable
and crashed.

SCARLET ANGEL

An Angel fell from her cloud.
Her wings of virtue tainted red.
The sinful skin she was wrapped in.
Didn't fit.... Or did it?
Once wholesome and pure.
Getting nowhere in love.
Her wings spread, her halo lost.
Torn between wrong and right.
Between dark and light.
The excitement of flying high.
Brought her down.
Caught in a fog. Undecided.
Until she saw the light
Inside herself.
And took flight.

EMOTIONAL QUICKSAND

Save me from myself.
I mean me no harm.
These tears I cry
soak the sands at my feet.
I find myself sinking.
The more I struggle
The deeper I get.
Suffocating.
There is no bottom.
No end to the tears.
Forever sinking in
murky clouds of confusion.
The healing sands of time.
I can pull myself out.
I still have the strength.
All I need to be saved,
is a steady hand to hold,
And the ability to trust it.

DOORMAT

You wiped your feet often.
Taking the mud from your day
And putting it on me.
Thinking that as time went by
and the mud dried...
I would just shake it off and
Wash it away.
My fibers strong.
It worked for a while.
Visibly clean on the surface,
I proved my resilience.
Day in day out.
But, for years the stains ran deep.
The dirt taking over my insides.
Until that is what I became.
Dirty.
Seeping from the inside out.
Vibrance lost
to an opaque surface.
The wear and tear prevailed.
I unraveled,
And the stains didn't matter.

I could never be clean again.
But, I could weave myself tighter-
with new threads of strength.
And refuse to just lie there,
Leaving you no place to wipe your feet.

BROKEN VOWS

I did not forsake all others, but you did,
our other vows that is.
I may have broken a vow. But then you did too.
Your promises to **love, honor,** and **cherish**
what happened?
Do you sign the paper and they perish?
Where was the **honor** in your high expectations?
Exceeded without gratitude or appreciation.
Only to be met with higher expectations. Of me.
Where was the **honor** in taking my hopes and dreams
and turning them into needless wants?
Because you lacked my ambition and were jealous of it.
Should I have felt **honored** that you thought I was strong
and could handle whatever you threw at me? And stay?
Eating crap politely with a smile.
Were you **cherishing** me when you endlessly made me cry?
Your angry outbursts and words that belittled and demeaned?
For no other reason but to take the stress off your day.
And try to put your weaknesses and faults on me.
Were you **cherishing** me at night? When I cried myself to sleep?
Watching your back as you snored in peace. Satiated by my body.
You had already let go of the day, but It was my time to reflect.
Wanting you but wanting out. Finding no peace for me.
Were you **cherishing** me by pushing me away? Closing me out.
Letting me think your unhappiness was my fault?
Did you think I would feel **loved** when you didn't **honor** or **cherish** me.
When you wouldn't **honor** my wish to be **cherished** and **loved**?
I told you what I needed, ignorance was no excuse. It's all I ever asked of you.
Were you **loving** me when I went the extra mile, trying to set the example.
And you threw it back in my face?

Did you watch me with adoring eyes, take every chance to touch me, to tell me I was beautiful or that you **love** me? Outside the bedroom that is? They lost their value there. For years you chose to break our vows. To **love, honor,** and **cherish.** I selfishly found those comforts in another. Our marriage handling its last reaming.

But, In losing us we found each other, and the reasons to change and make us work.

We owned our mistakes and realized… the most important vows… For better or worse, til death do us part—to us, have always held their meaning.

EXIT AFFAIR

I was on my way out.
Thinking he wouldn't stay,
Once he found out I would stray.
I didn't have the heart to
leave on my own.
To take his babies miles away.
Where my life was before him.
Where my people live.
I didn't hate him enough.
I didn't love him enough.
I couldn't keep living that way.
I had no other reason .
Leave first they say, before you stray.
But is it really that easy?
I was making a choice
for both of us.
Neither his choosing.
Either way he'd be losing.
And I didn't hate him enough
or love him enough.
To keep living that way.

ISSUES

Dancing around
never facing
perceptions in themselves
struggling with the waste
finding themselves shelved
Peeking briefly, then all out
from their hiding place
dancing around once again
though they never face
intentions known.to no avail
its easier to dance or hide
once again resolve shelved
in face of to much pride.

Crossing The Line

"I've crossed the last line from where I can't return where
every step I took in faith betrayed me and led me from my home."
—Sarah Mclachlan

At The Coffee Shop

Watching you watch me
through the panes of glass.
Your interest intrigues me.
Staring over your coffee cup
from the cab of the truck.
Subtly trying to be subtle.
Without success.
I hear the register ringing,
my change singing
as I pay.
You drive away.
Slowly. Eyes following.
Hinting excitement
of what could be.
Coffee steaming, energizing.
My mind rhythms to a new beat.
There shouldn't be a dance,
but I'm so tempted...
In my new found selfishness.
My character put to the test.
Not passing.
A pause of low morality.
I blame it on the caffeine.
I should look the other way
And keep the glass between.

ROLLER COASTER RIDE

Take this ride with me?
Is it safe?
There are no guarantees.
Will there be a lot of
ups and downs?
You will just have to see.
Will I be hanging on for dear life?
Don't worry I will protect you.
Will my life be turned upside down?
Just hang on tight.
What if I let go?
I will hold you against me.
What if I want off?
All you have to do is ask.
Who decides when the way splits?.
We can do that together.
Will someone get hurt?
There is a chance.
Is it worth the risk?
Yes, I think so;
We will feel spontaneous and
exhilarated during the ups,
Confused and sad in the downs.
The twist and turns
will scare us,
As well as the unknown.
We will hang on so long.
We wont know how to let go.
When we want to get off.
We will wait a spell.

Then want back on.
Even if we feel butterflies.
We will question our judgment.
For taking the risk.
Then validate our feelings.
With the rush.
So
Take this ride with me?

FIRST TIME

Do you remember that first time
in the broad of day?
Surrounded by whispering trees
and the lingering scent of
sweet mowed hay.
Your eyes focused intently on mine.
Your smile shy and unsure.
Neither wanting to be made the fool.
Our first kiss held the answer.
Sweet and tender we tasted,
tentative then we indulged.
Like a succulent dessert not to
be wasted.
Secrets not to be divulged.
You asked to see my tattoo.
It's in a sensual place.
Leaning down to kiss it.
An image I will never replace.
You wandered to the petal folds
that waited for your touch.
Your breath blowing the soft down.
The moist warmth caressed so much.
Your hands cupped me lovingly,
while your fingers dared explore.
All I could think that moment was
more please, sweet surrender, more.
When we were down to the bare
your eyes never leaving mine.
I saw into your soul that day.
As you entered my divine.

The rush, the fullness, the feelings.
We got lost in ecstasies throes.
We came in euphoric melody
The curling of my toes.
It was hard to say good bye that day.
After we had crossed that line.
We belonged to others.
For that moment you were mine.

MID LIFE RIPPLES

There comes a time
In the middle of a mans life
When the quiet lake
he found comfort in,
suddenly becomes too calm,
almost stagnant.
He dreams of ocean waves
and river cascades.
He yearns to prove himself
ready for a new adventure.
He throws a pebble in the water
causing ripples in his reflection.
They excite him, entice him,
encouraging him to throw larger stones.
The raised flow higher and longer lasting.
So he continues; distorting his image until
he's not even recognizable to himself.
Each stone larger than the one before.
Making the ripples so forceful,
they have become the waves he longed for.
Eventually he plays out all his energy,
The heavy stones weighing him down.
He knows he should stop but he denies.
He is addicted to the emotional arousal-
the feeling of power and pride.
He imagines the lake anticipates each pebble.
The waves needing him to exist and flourish.
His ego boosted, his importance proved.
Then nature plays its consequences.

His confidence is taken from him.
The waves he so fondly roused turn tides.
Threaten to take away his control.
To suck him in and pull him under.
He realizes almost to late
that he started an adventure he was
not prepared to endure.
The risks were greater than his faith.
He finds the strength in fear to retreat.
But not completely.
He admires the diminishing waves from afar
as he waits for the lake to regain its calm.
Carefully holding a pebble in his palm.

MORNING ROUTINE

Slowly lifting covers
gently touching feet to floor.
Quiet, so quiet.
For a sweet moment
I watch him sleep.
The peaceful breathing.
There is no anger in his slumber.
If he could be awake like this.
Calm and peaceful.
Its to late for me to wish.
I'm all out of tears.
Our connection gone.
I can't remember having one.
He stirs in my quiet attempt
to dress.
"Shh…Im going to the gym."
It comes so easily.
He nods his head and
cuddles deep in cover.
My morning routine.
Nothing is amiss.
I grab my gym bag and
Head out the door.
Glancing back to the
man that I long ago wed.
He hasn't noticed,
in recent months,
My gym shoes stayed
under the bed.

MY SHADOW

Oh, if you could talk
What stories you'd tell.
Watching from the wall, the truck.
From the timber trail.
Living through me. With me.
Your senses reeling at my antics.
Do I make you blush a rosy hue-
Against your eternal shades of gray?
A sunset in the dusk of naughty trysts.
Mimicking my every move.
Out of proportion, sensual and slow.
An erotic play in the light of day.
Only the sun will know.

SLOW RUSH

Painted nails skimming new skin,
Waiting to be explored.
Soft but weathered with age.
The plush hair across his chest
arouses my breast.
Nipples anticipating the wet
silk of his tongue.
His mouth on mine.
A taste unique to him,
coffee hiding a hint of beer.
To early in the morn for approval.
He isn't mine. That worry is hers.
Looking into eyes never wavering.
The intimacy of it.
Mirrors of my emotion.
A fresh look at love.
So reassuring.
How can this be wrong?
His palms caress my bottom
pulling me closer, deeper.
Reaching the core of me.
A heated climax; Saying my name.
He's with only me at this moment.
Exhaling with the claim of love.
Shaking knees hold him over me.
But barely.
Its so right, this feeling.
This passionate infatuation.
Until my handle on reality
Opens the door.

VALENTINE NOTE

I don't believe in 'soul mates'...or that there is just
one person in this world for everyone.
But.
I do believe that one person can get so deep into your
soul that they consume your heart and impassion your mind,
changing your life forever.
Thank you for burning into my soul and giving me the gift
of our love, even though it will be considered just a
blink in my lifetime. My eyes have been opened for eternity.
No matter what our tomorrow brings, I will treasure our
yesterdays.

CHRISTMAS GOODBYE SONG

Meet me underneath the mistletoe.
One last kiss she doesn't have to know.
Take me underneath the Christmas tree.
I'll unwrap you carefully.
The lights soft glows glistenin'
as we lie together skin to skin.

Meet me underneath the mistletoe.
One last kiss she doesn't have to know.
Let me love you just one last time.
I'll pretend that you're all mine.
Let this be your last gift to me.
Underneath the Christmas tree.

Meet me underneath the mistletoe.
One last kiss she doesn't have to know.
Meet me underneath the mistletoe
One last kiss and then I have to go.

A COWGIRLS PLEASURE

In awe of the rush,
The powerful muscle
between her thighs.
She holds on tight.
Salty, leathery sweat
lingers in the air.
So thick she can taste it.
Nostrils flared, labored breathing.
Pounding, pounding,
ground vibrates underneath.
He asks for head, She gives it.
Steady hands hold nothing back.
Poetry in motion.
Thundering emotion.
They move as one.
Striding toward new horizons.
He takes them further,
But its never far enough.
Hearts about to burst.
Blood pumping rhythmic,
to a sinful energetic tune.
Sun rays casts shadows,
two stepping with the tree tops.
Their escapade slows to
watch the lazy world settle.
Calming, Cautioning.
A prelude to the end.
Its bittersweet reality.
Her feelings bona fide.
She longs for the trail
but lives for the ride.

ADDICTION

She finds her happiness
on the outside.
He's out there like a drug.
Preying on those weak in their need,
Vulnerable in their wants.
He makes himself irresistible
while pushing his charms his promises.
If she could just say no.
Deny the temptation.
But she wants her joy
and an end to her pain.
It's so easy to take what's offered.
Available in secrecy.
She crosses the line.
Sucked in to the surreal world.
Held their captive in it.
Her addiction to the illusions.
She looks forward to her fix.
Nothing matters but her need.
Seeing, feeling, tasting, loving.
Learning to lie and manipulate.
Almost losing herself.
So secure in her happiness,
she starts demanding more than
he can spare.
He cuts her back slowly.
Weaning.
He cant let her go cold turkey.
Giving her just enough to keep
her hooked.
To keep her in his hand.
He supplements with another drug;
Anger, denial, deceit.

This is her undoing.
Her body rejects it,
goes through withdrawal.
Dying inside. She feels it.
Coming out of denial,
She finds the strength in family.
To purge him from her system.
Detox, rehabilitate and heal.
Learning the addicting causes.
Looking for the signs.
Power through knowledge.
Promotion through awareness.
He will be taken out of commission
He won't so easily prey again.

WALLS

A wall goes up around my heart
Keeping it protected and secure.
With every mean word spoken,
every intent to hurt or demean,
another brick gets laid.
Mortared by resentment.
On occasion, with a kind word-
a compliment or support,
One brick falls.
Then more disrespect and anger.
Three go up.
The process continues.
One brick down, three bricks up.
My heart refuses to keep hurting.
The wall strengthens but
not without its faults.
Opportunity presents itself.
Another builder preys on the
walls weaknesses.
He chisels away the mortar with
charm, hope, value, and inspiration.
The wall slowly crumbles.
Trusting that I wont be invaded with
darkness;
My heart lets down its guard
to take in the light.
Wanting to build a new structure
with a foundation of love, respect,
adoration and happiness.
Secure in its foolish trust.
Leaving itself vulnerable and open.
New lies, deceit and betrayal.

My unprotected heart is
emotionally crushed.
Left with just enough strength
to start a new wall.
Going back to the original builder.
Seeking to restructure.
But he has changed his plans.
He accepted his errors in the old wall.
Wanting to make things right.
Encourages me to heal from the inside.
To feel secure in my own skin
with love, respect, admiration
learning to trust again.
And keep the walls down.

SWEET LITTLE LIES

Tell me lies, sweet little lies.
Tell me again that you are in love with me.
But you also love your wife.
That no one has ever made you feel like this
when I question why you stray.
Tell me that I am worth the risk.
When you know all you stand to lose.
That you will always love me dearly,
Even if we part.
Tell me that you want to take me to Jamaica
and see me topless on the beach.
Tell me that you want to take me to that concert
when we listen to the same band.
Tell me that you value me as a parent
because you know I put them before you.
Tell me that you respect me as a person
knowing my flaws and weaknesses.
Tell me how much you miss me
though we just talked an hour before.
Tell me that I make you laugh.
When we start the day with smiles.
Tell me how you dream of me at three A.M.
and you are laying next to your wife.
Tell me that you wake up thinking about me
and go to bed the same way.
Tell me how you smell me on you
when you sit in a bank meeting daydreaming.
That you feel my presence without seeing,
when you sense I'm near.
Tell me how jealous you get
when I go out with my husband.
Tell me how you worry about me
when I run away for the day without calling.

Tell me that you talk to me more than anyone, ever.
When we share our secrets.
Tell me I'm an incredible, intimate lover,
when your knees start shaking at the thought.
Tell me how special we are together.
While giving reasons why.
Tell me that we will still be together in five years.
And that we will always have this connection.
And that you don't want to go on vacation
Because of how much you'll miss me.
Tell me how proud you are of my accomplishments
when you know you supported me.
Tell me that you never want me mad at you.
When you feel like I am drifting.
Tell me that you can't let me go.
Every time I try to cut ties.
Tell me once more how you cried on your tractor.
When I ended us the first time.
Tell me that I wasn't your mid life crisis.
when I tried to understand.
Tell me how I cut you off at the knees
when I said you should have bought the Beamer.
(For his mid life crisis)
Tell me that your obligated to save your marriage
but can't get me out of your head.
Tell me again and again that you won't hurt me
Even though I know you will.
You were telling me lies, sweet little lies.
So.
Tell me, what are you telling her?

DISCONNECTED

Oh husband of mine
How can you not see?
Are we connected at all?
She knew right off.
She is so in tune.
I'm jealous in a way.
That he has that
and I don't.
You see only the surface.
Which I keep plastic.
Like a Stepford wife.
But if you knew me
the woman inside.
You'd know I'm drifting.
That another has my soul.
She does.
She pries, sorts and stores.
In waiting.
She knows his past.
Her trust nonexistent.
You trust so blindly.
My pedestal so high.
It's wrong to take advantage.
Or you don't want to see?
How. How can you not feel it?
That my mind is consumed,
my heart impassioned.
It's crazy to wish you did.
Then my freedom would be limited.
And you would be hurting
because of me.
But I wish it.
I wish for you to wonder.

To feel that something is wrong.
So that when it all comes out.
When I confess to save us.
I feel there is some foundation
for us to build on.
Should we chose too.
They will. They will build.
She has enabled for years.
A party to his infidelity.
Our past is clean
but our future is tainted.
They deserve each other.
Do we?

COMING TO TERMS:

"His wrongs don't make me right"
—NJR

EXPLAINING WHY

When you thought all was lost
because in her heart she knew.
I heard your sadness and defeat
I realized it was true.

She was the one you needed.
I would never be enough.
I knew I had to let you go.
The way I chose was tough.

She had to have something to
validate her woman's intuition.
Lying and denying us
did not help the situation.

So what I believe was out of love,
I found a way to give you hope.
I told her the rumors weren't true.
But there was something to the scope.

I made light of our relationship
Claiming we were just good friends.
Never loving, never touching,
For you I tried to make amends.

I broke my heart to pieces
with every; HE loves YOU.
That I was just a friend.
Was that part even true?

She seemed to be placated.
Having something now concrete.
A foundation for you to build on.

While I step back and retreat.

I defended and protected you
while I tried to prove my love.
Without a thank you or a screw you
you bailed when push came to shove.

But what hurts the worst in all of this
Is how you let them lie.
They don't know me, but you do
and you believed without deny.

But I think you know deep down
what is really true.
I put my marriage on the line;
to save yours.
All because I loved you.

UNDERSTANDING ME

You didn't understand what I meant when I said "I Love You."
What I meant was;
While you adore, respect, admire, honor, cherish,
and protect me.
I will do the same for you with passion.
Until you hurt me.
You didn't understand what I meant when I said, "You're my
best friend."
What I meant was;
I will keep your secrets, support your goals, cover your lies,
trust your honesty, share your laughs, and shoulder your fears.
Until you hurt me.
You didn't understand what I meant when
I said "You know me, all of me, completely."
What I meant was;
I never hid myself from you. I'm a good person, a loyal friend,
a loving mother, a compassionate woman, a unique individual.
And STRONG.
I bend but I don't break, I make mistakes but try to mend them,
I hurt but I heal, When life throws me. I will dust myself off
and cowgirl up.
And God help you if you hurt me.

SECRET SMILES

Secret smile.
Just for us.
Sweet lies become.
A double betrayal.
Lying to her to keep me.
Lying to me to keep me.
Why?
In the beginning you wanted her.
In the end you want her.
Save my heart, spare my soul.
Should have kept it tangible
not emotional.
Your mid life addiction.
You could have used me without-
Love.
You could have let me go without-
Hate.
You control her with lies.
She allows it.
You push me away with the truth.
I retreat sadly.
She forgives because she doesn't understand.
Not completely.
But I do. I know too well.
I will not forgive or forget.
The truth will heal me.
Cleanse my conscience.

Lies will endanger your soul.
You encourage this
You keep on;
Lying, denying.
Your conscience diseased.
I owned my mistakes.
I will heal. I will be whole.
I will wonder who that
man was.
The one I learned was a coward.
Who shattered my heart.
Leaving me to put the pieces
together.
In time they all fit.
I find myself again.
Stronger now. Whole
Safe in trusting myself.
I embrace my new spirit with
A secret smile.
Just for me.

GAMES

We played a game that nobody wins.
You were the expert,
But you went outside the rules.
You started with the 'what ifs',
the 'dreaming out loud'.
You got caught up in your emotions.
But your need to be in control,
took away your freedom to play for real.
I was learning as I went.
My questions causing you distress.
To be honest with me,
You had to be honest with yourself.
Then you would lose your advantage.
And the game would be fair.
So you cheated and I called you on it.
Your sportsmanship proved lacking.
In the end. It's a tie. We both lost.

FORBIDDEN LOVE

Its like trying out a new dessert.
You want to taste it, savor it,
cherish every bite.
So rich its sinful.
Its bad for you but so tempting.
You deny what it will do.
The cravings overwhelm your mind.
You look for every chance to relish it.
The fix to your sweet tooth.
You keep it a secret from others.
Overeating becoming a disease.
Consuming out of control.
It starts to make you sick.
The richness that drew you to it,
now settling unwell in your stomach.
You want to purge it.
Remove it from your system.
To work off all the damage caused.
Tell others to keep you away from it.
You avoid where its served.
In time the cravings lessen.
You remember how sick it made you
when the cravings return.
And the temptations gone.
You won't indulge again.

SEASONS OF INFIDELITY

The beauty forever. A quiet leeway
lined with trees.
The quiet equine eyes behind the fence,
a constant reminder we were
never really alone.
The trees, full in their summer foliage,
blocked the view of the road.
Hiding our liaisons from passer byes.
The corn, green with strong stalk, reached
for the suns inspiration.
The wind whispered through its broad leaf
in a calming shush, shush.
The birds sang in full tune. Invading each
others private moments.
We were in full bloom with the nature around us.

The Autumn chills came. The leaves transformed
to reds and golds. Vibrant and beautiful.
A gentle reminder that life is ever changing.
The corn, having reached its full potential, drys in
preparation for harvest. The cool fall breeze soothed
through the withered leaves in a crisp ghostly whisper.
Birds sang their good byes. The nests abandoned.
We followed natures course. Our love changing.

Winter winds blew the leaves from the trees.
Hollow branches waving their icy hellos.
The road visible to us from all angles.
An easy see for those passing by.
Equine friends took on plush fur,
still ever watching,

through a sparkling fence line.
The corn long since turned to back to seed.
The ground tilled through old stalk.
A snowy blanket of solitude. Life not meant to
weather the harsh cold, died. As our love did.

There will be no Spring for us.
We won't watch the corn shoots tease the soil
with the promise of growth.
Or the trees budding with hopes of fresh
protection from the roads view.
We won't hear the birds singing to their mates,
Or observe the fledglings come to life.
Waiting to say hello.
There will be no renewal or growth for us.
Just fond memories of seasons past.
We will never have our spring.
But we will always have our spot.

I MISS MY LOVER

I miss my lover.
Like a calm ocean misses a wave.
Waiting in quiet expectation.
The heart of the swell builds
with spontaneity.
Rising higher with its passion.
The foam lovingly caressing the surface
until it gets lost in itself.
Carrying with it treasures
to be secret keepsakes forever.
The stormy times are best.
The waves continuous,
overpowering and dangerous.
Not without control or consequence.
Like our loving.
The climax is over as the wave
hits the shore.
Retreating back into itself.
Lulled to it comforts.
The ocean is quiet once more.
Waiting for the next storm
I miss my lover.

HE SAID...HE MEANT

He said:
I can't handle rejection. I don't like to be made a fool of.
He meant:
I do the playing. You are the fool.
I'm sucking you in by expressing a vulnerability.
He said:
I tell you more than anyone else. Ever.
He meant:
I tell you more than the last woman I told this too.
He said:
I'm in love with you. I don't want to let you go.
He meant:
I love that you love me. It strokes my ego.
He said:
If this was a mid life crisis I would have bought the Beamer.
He meant:
My wife wouldn't let me buy it.
He said:
Don't try to get into my head.
He meant:
If you knew what I really thought. You would run.
I don't own my actions
He said:
DO NOT tell your husband about us.
He meant:
I will deny, deny, deny. And cover my own ass.
You will be on your own.
He said:
It won't come out because I assume you won't say anything.
He meant:
I know you love me too much to ever hurt me.
I'm counting on it.

He said:
You meant nothing. You don't know me.
He meant:
(Back to the beginning)
I am the player. You are the fool.

WATCHING ME

I daydreamed again that
I was sitting at the park
alone, under a tree.
You were watching secretly.
From afar.
Wondering how
I could look so alone,
After all this time.
How even in the vibrant sun,
My light was gone.
Blown out by betrayal.
You miss seeing it.
That inner light.
Shown through a smile.
Or bright eyes.
Accenting my outer beauty.
It always warmed your soul.
But your soul is cold now.
Because of the darkness
you put in mine.
I glanced your way.
Unseeing but feeling.
I sensed you close.
I looked down.
To hide the tears.
Just in case you can see.
You can't have that power back.
Where you can see me cry.
Alone in the park under a tree.
I don't want you watching me.
Not until I can smile again.

SAVING MYSELF

I have this vision—
that I'm drowning in dark waters
and you are watching from the shore.
You don't try to help me.
Because you can't swim.
You're scared that by hanging on to you
I will take you under.
You stand there observing
as I call out your name.
Reaching for you.
Going under but fighting to resurface.
Again and again.
You hold your place.
Because you can't swim.
Never searching for a life line,
never asking for help.
Ignoring any options to save me.
They surround you but you deny.
All you know is you can't swim.
When I go under for the last time
when the life is squeezed out of me.
Then I am gone to you.
I can't come back.
You can move on without me,
But you will live with the guilt
that you could have saved me.
If you had been brave enough.

Don't turn your back too soon.
I will find the strength to survive.
When I get to my lowest point;
To the darkest recess of my soul.
Finding direction in the glow above,
When I touch rock bottom.
I will push off the waters floor.
Surface again and learn to swim.
I will save myself.
All on my own.
And maybe push you in.

COWGIRL UP

Jeans hung low, hips swaying to her own beat.
Her belt buckle, once shiny, now tarnished with wear.
Her hat, angled ragged across her brow,
shades her eyes from passer byes.
She rarely goes unnoticed and misses nothing.
Her shirt tied up and contouring from humidity.
The word 'Dangerous' across her chest. Subtly warning.
The sun reflecting light off of the gem in her navel.
Adding a delicate touch to a tough demeanor.
Tan skin covered in bruises and scrapes.
Make no mistake, she won't break.
She can take a good bucking, and if she gets thrown.
She will land with her boots running.
Because you can't keep a Cowgirl down.
Not for long.
Unless you find a way into her heart.
Anyone can love her from afar, but she won't love easy.
When she finds one thought worthy.
She'll give 100% like she does everything else.
Her body can take a beating. A broken heart still beats.
Black and blue. Another bruise to heal.
So when she's played—when her pride shatters.
She'll lay low til she finds her good n pissed.
If you're the cause, she'll be relentless.
It would be wise to saddle up quick and ride away.
Before she Cowgirls Up.

Full Confessions

"A strong woman heals from the whole truth within her not the half truths given to her."

HUSH LITTLE MISTRESS

Hush Little Mistress
It's not smart of you to snub.
Heed this gentle warning
from the Good Ole Boys Club.

Hush Little Mistress
Now don't you tell.
So he played your heart
and put you through hell.

Hush Little Mistress
don't cross that line.
Keep your mouth shut
everything will be fine.

Hush Little Mistress
You should know your place.
If this gets around
Oh, the problems you'll face.

Hush Little Mistress
You are not one of us.
We will accept and support him
His business a plus.

Hush Little Mistress
Telling will only get you hurt.
We will always protect him
And treat you like dirt.

Hush Little Mistress
He has done this before.
If he pulls it off again,
There will be many more.

Hey Little Mistress
You just had to snitch.
Now people know he's a Dog
And he screwed the wrong bitch.

THE BITCH

You kicked me when I was down.
Thinking I would run and hide,
crawl in a hole and lick my wounds.
But I am not that kind.
I won't take it lying down.
I am not submissive.
If you hurt me I will turn on you.
Full force…
And bite you on the ass.
Leaving a bad taste in my mouth.

TELLING HER EVERYTHING

I'm sorry to have to be the one
That tells you about the lies.
I wanted him to face you in truth
but he still avoids and denies.

I know he says you're crazy,
That you couldn't be more wrong.
While he sang to me, a new tune.
A whole different kind of song.

It's not fair how he's played us.
I can't enable it anymore.
I have the balls to face you.
And tell you there was more.

I'm now an open book.
So much that you need to know.
He refuses to own his claim to love me,
and that is the lowest blow.

I'm coming to you as a woman,
He has hurt with false intent.
You have walked in my shoes.
You know what it all meant.

He and I talked a thousand hours.
Shared naked moments in passion.
When I came to you the first time—
He lost all his compassion.

I went to him for closure.
The strings we left in knots.
He crudely gave me my answers.
He thinks he's calling all the shots.

He told me months of loving
meant nothing, a mistake.
That is a hard pill to swallow.
All he wanted was his cake.

I get to live with falling
for the oldest trick in the book.
But you get to live with him.
I'm getting off his hook.

I'm wishing you the best
I think you will need it in the end.
I'm sorry for my part in hurting you.
Now I have my home to mend.

THE OTHER WOMAN BOND

I'd say before you judge,
walk a mile in my shoes.
But, you have taken this path
before me.
You thought you were different.
And maybe you are.
But he is not.
He hasn't changed.
There were many before you with her.
Many before me with you.
We were not exclusive.
Hate me if you must,
for what I have done.
As she must have hated you,
for doing the same.
We compared notes, you and I.
And he used the same lines.
We are similar
in that we fell for them.
So different our ending.
You got his ring.
I left the dance.
If he cheats with you.
He'll cheat on you.
I wouldn't take that chance.

FACING REALITY

I did not want to know you
You weren't a real person to me
Just a character in his life story
And that was fine with me.

All the faces he put on you.
I could only imagine to be.
I didn't know your true expressions.
That worked well for me.

You could be the bitch
who nagged at him all day.
Or the conservative prude
who refused to wear lingerie.

You could be the loving wife
that did everything for him.
Or the one who spent all the money,
always shopping on a whim.

You could make him feel neglected
or be perfect in every way.
All depending on precisely-
how he wanted me to think of you that day.

I didn't want to know you
But that was not meant to be
And now that we've met
You are very real to me, and I'm sorry.

I have learned that you are kind
and have amazing strength within.
Confronting adversity with compassion.
Your faces shouldn't come from him.

THAT WOULD BE ME

Who takes a life
and makes a choice
to shatter its dreams, its realities?
Who takes blind trust
and abuses it
to enable lies and deceit?
Who takes a love so pure
It's unseen by the naked eye
and taints it to visibility?
Who lowers her morals
for a rush, for selfish desires
from insecurity?
Who disrespects her family
causing so much pain
because she was unhappy?
Who has the mind to compartmentalize
to take two loves and keep them separate
thinking they would never meet?
Who loves and loses by her choices alone?
That would be me.

ONE HEALING BREATH

Lungs aflame.
My heart in cautioned pause.
Craving oxygen.
Forgetting how to breathe.
In and out, for survival sake.
My mouth opens and closes.
Like a fish suffocating in air.
As I try to tell. And falter.

Breathe just breathe.
It's unjust to tear out a heart
so trusting and alive.
Is this premeditated murder?
Knowing my words will kill
the very life we live.
His thoughtful gaze questioning.
A worried brow creases
In understanding and acceptance.
It's the calm before the storm.
Breathe just breathe.
Buying time. One more moment.
Of the life I'm living.
Before he takes it away.
I can't tell him, I won't.
I don't want to be brave.
But I must, It has to be done.
So we can try to move on.
I've never been a coward.
I inhale deeply,
stretching my lungs,
painfully holding. Stalling.
My conscience aches for air.
I exhale slowly,
months of infidelity out
In one long freeing breath.
I watch as he takes it all in.
My air of secrets.
And stops.
His tears fall on skin
tainting blue.
Falling into my arms
as I whisper encouragement,
Breathe Baby, just breathe.

RAW BONED HONESTY

Proving commitment
has eaten away my flesh.
Leaving me raw and exposed.
Every lie, every omission revealed.
Waiting it out as I spilled my guts.
Watching in morbid curiosity
as the layers of truth ripped
through me.
All that is left is bone and organ.
My protective covering gone.
Nothing left to hide my secrets.
The damage to my heart visible.
My structure strong.
In awe of my tortured reality.
Proof of love and devotion.
to him-
At my most grotesque,
my most vulnerable.
I was never more beautiful.

HE KNOWS

Running.
As hard as I can.
This body can't take anymore.
Muscles burning from the strain.
Punishing myself.
My heart ready to explode.
This is what I've done to him.
My chest heaving for air.
He feels this tenfold.
That his heart will burst.
Faster, faster.
The demons chase.
There is no where to go
that they can't follow.
It's hard to tell the tears
from the sweat.
But I see clearly.
I feel his pain.
I can't stop-
Running.

SOMEDAY

The door chimes in greeting.
Echoing in his mind.
The wood planks thunder
in his rage.
Weapons of hardware surround him.
Safely untouched.
His hands will prevail.
Patrons survey with excited eyes.
Eager to wag their tongues.
Feigning interest in old merchandise,
The tools of their trade.
They go unnoticed.
His focus on one. Only one
The man brave enough to hold his wife.
To stick the knife in his back,
but lacking the integrity to face him.
Forewarned this mans intent,
The coward departed.
His walls of safety invaded.
His people left to cover,
If they will.
They know his infidelities, his wrongs.
The aggressor calms with avoidance.
Suppressed by the other mans weakness.
The reality of his actions unsettling.
He removes himself of his own accord.
Plans thwarted but his intent known.
Someday. Someday.

LOST BALLS

What happened to your balls?
I know you had them.
I have seen them,
even held them in my hand.
It took balls to sleep with me.
The wife of another man.
To tell me you love me
and buy me gifts.
What happened to them?
Did they shrivel up in confrontation?
Making it easier for you to run?
You need to find your balls.
So you can own your life,
quit denying and make amends.
If you can't get them back, let me know.
I have a set you can borrow.

BE FREE

I was your heaven .
And now I am your hell.
I can't make you chose the right path.
But I can be a constant reminder of
the consequences.
When you think that you are superior.
That you have the right to dispose.
Your road will be a long and lonely one.
When you chose the same paths that
take you nowhere;
I will be the little voice in your head
telling you to reconsider.
Temptation is the short easy road.
The long road to redemption is your freedom.
It's your choice.
Take the high road for once.
Be free.

DOG AT LARGE

Mothers warn your daughters
Husbands hold on to your wives.
He's escaped his ball and chain.
At it once again.
On the prowl.
Needing to feed his hunger.
Sniffing skirts, marking new territory.
A menace to the community.
Someone should call his home.
Tell her he's at large again.
So she can take him back in.
Like she always does.
She thought he learned his lesson.
But he will always want to stray.
There is only one way to keep him.
Get him neutered and he will stay.

THE CROSSWALK

You look so small
stepping off the curb.
Cautiously crossing my path.
Worry not old lover.
Just stay between the lines.
You are nothing to me.
Once thought so big and important.
But I have seen all sides.
You are not as you appear.
The mask you wear for the public
is invisible to me now.
A real man has honor in his word.
You can not be trusted.
I have been exposed to
the sugar coated venom you spew.
I am immune now.
Reality is my antidote.
You have proven you are weak.
Leaving marks on the ones
who loved you.
Mentally and physically.
Someday everyone will see
you for what you are.
Unless you are too small.

Healing Thoughts

"Perhaps love is the process of leading you back to yourself."

CORNER OF MY HEART

In the corner of my heart
sits a memory
a vision of life yet to pass
It sits there diligently
taunting me
The part that is cold and vast
I wish for it to go away
But it's where it needs to be
A reminder of pain I've caused.
My corner of accountability.

LYING IN THE BED I MADE

I'm tired of being a flower
In a garden of weeds.
It takes so much energy to bloom.
It's restful being a bud
closed up in protection.
Please don't water me
with false inspiration.
Or encourage me to grow
with bullshit.
I don't want to open up.
To stretch my roots or
Show my true colors.
Only to be compared to the weeds.
I bed with.

EMOTIONAL SECURITY

Lock yourself safely.
Don't let anyone in.
Security is the key
to protection.
If you leave yourself open.
They will invite themselves in.
Breaking and taking,
the things you consider valuable.
Then they will leave,
shutting the door behind them.
Never looking back.
Leaving you to clean up the mess.

KNOWING YOURSELF

How well do you know yourself.
Your level of darkness, your limits?
Do you know how long you can paddle
in an ocean alone?
How long you can keep your head above water,
before sinking and finding comfort in drowning.
How long can you last in a box, in quiet darkness.
Touching walls that seem to close in, without escape.
Before you snap and give in to the darkness?
Do you know?
Do you know how you would feel about the person
that came to your rescue?
That reached in and pulled you out of the water,
Giving you a reason to breathe.
The person that took away the walls holding you in
and showed you light in the darkness.
Who held you and told you that you were special.
Would you love that person with all your heart?
How would you feel in the end?
When he put you back in the box and threw you alone
into the ocean. Sinking. Leaving you drowning in darkness.
Trying to save yourself.
Would you realize he was bad all along? That he
only saved you for his own pleasures.
And that when he was done, you would be worse off
than you were before?
Do you know yourself well enough to say-
That you would never find yourself in the ocean alone,
or in locked in a box of darkness?
That you will never need to be saved?
I thought I knew myself.
I never say never

HINDSIGHT

I see her face,
In flashes of pain and confusion.
It saddens me.
A broken sisterhood of sorts, tho
before then we'd never met.
I told too much. In hindsight.
She wanted to know but not.
I needed to purge my demons.
Give them to her to give back to him.
It doesn't work that way.
Now we all carry them.
But there is a blessin' in every lesson.
I found out all I needed I have at home.
She doesn't need what she has at home.
Eyes wide open. Yet, she stays.
It saddens me.
That she lives that way.
In pain and confusion.
In hindsight.
Too much came from me.

RUNNING ON EMPTY

I'm running on empty.
I always thought if I won millions,
I would share my wealth with others.
Because no one person needs that much.
I had a lotto of love inside me.
I had more.
Than any one person needed.
I no longer care to share.
What little is left.
Had I only known.
I'm learning from the world around me.
Take and you shall receive.
Give and they will leave.
It's that easy.

GREENER GRASSES

I was sitting on the fence
trying to decide,
If the grass is really greener
on the other side.
On the side that I was living
a patch of weeds did grow.
The side that I longed for
someone else had come to mow.
The weeds were constantly taking
what the grass needed to nourish.
The grass on the other side,
consistent in its flourish.
There was history on my side.
Years of nurturing every blade.
The other side had bright beginnings.
But not without its share of shade.
So I sat there and I pondered.
Till I fell off on my ass.
I landed on the greener side.
It wasn't really grass!
Its brightness uniform,
Its height always mowed so neat.
It sure was pretty to look at
but I wouldn't walk it with bare feet.
The texture was too rough,
so plastic in its feel.
Astro turf laid for appearance sake.

None of it was real.
Its beauty on the surface
but when I pulled a corner back.
Underneath there was a coldness.
The insides were asphalt black.
I hopped back on the fence
gaining a new splinter.
Is it greener on the other side?
It will be in the winter!
Would that be what I wanted?
A false life without weeds?
Where there is no renewal of growth
where I planted all the seeds.
The Astro turf self sustaining.
What would it need me for?
I would lose the value in myself
and my desire to do more.
So I will keep the side I'm living.
Work on removing all the weeds.
By watering the grass around me
and planting greener seeds.

MYTH OF HEART

Myth of heart
a story untold
trying to explain
the need to hold
the want for pleasure
the fear of pain
Cautioned appearance
living in vain

Myth of heart
the giving of soul
learning to listen
allowing a goal
showing acceptance
willing to trust
physical attraction
intellectual lust

Myth of heart
the meaning of love
proving of loyalty
when push comes to shove
open affection
emotionally pure
Myth of heart.
How can we be sure?

HEALING

My body is lead
against the sheet.
Getting out of bed
is no small feat.
Once I feel the floor
there is no retreat.
I have to face the day.
I don't want to be numb.
If I get outside
I will feel the sun.
My face will soak
up the rays.
I will say.
Today is the day.
I will forget to cry.
I will find my light.
My options are as endless
as the sky is bright.
I will succeed.
I will prosper.
Then I will dread the night
and all it offers.
It will bring back the memories.
I will wake up feeling blue.
But I will get out of that bed
As each day starts anew.

WILL I?

Sometimes I wake up and think;
Today I am going to jump off that bridge
to see if I will fly or fall.
If I fly,
How far will I go before falling?
If I fall,
Will I land in a way that
I can dust myself off, climb up that bridge
and try to fly again?

GOING THROUGH THE MOTIONS

Lying in bed,
The strain from nights dreams
Weighing heavily.
The covers thrown over my head to drown out the light.
Suffocating in the sweet scent of vanilla.
A prison of sorts, one I don't want to leave.
For that is where I should be.
Dreams, intangible dreams.
Where everything I have is slipping away
and everything I want is just out of reach.
Crying but I can't feel the tears. I can't feel anything.
I want to feel but there is security in numbness.
Comfort in the darkness.
Not wanting to die, but not scared of dying,
and that thought alone scares me.
But I have to turn on the light and get moving.
Kids of to school and work to be done.
A spouse needing reassured.
People in their nosiness pretending to care.
I just want to get through the day, with my plastic
smile and happy facade.
Without any triggers, or moments, or yearnings.
Go through the motions and get everything done.
So I can get back into this bed, put the covers over my head.
Only to start all over again in the morning.

ANSWERS

I look to the sky
and ask the clouds
why loving is so wrong.

I asked the birds
why I'm living this hell.
They didn't sing their song.

In the night
I asked the moon
how one could hurt me so.

The stars would
twinkle against the night
and still I do not know.

I asked the earth
the reason why
I'm being punished so greatly.

The ocean waves
couldn't comfort me
I can't find the answers lately.

As a last resort
I went to God
since his nature didn't stir.

I could feel in me
His sympathy
but I still don't have the answer.

EVER AGAIN?

What if
you never again get the chance
to feel euphoric love?
The love that takes your heart
And removes it from your body.
Far away from your conscience
So they can't communicate.
The love that takes your soul
and wraps it around your wayward heart.
Dancing playfully.
Always just out of reach.
Testing your spirit and determination.
If you could just grab a hold of the aura
and consume its light.
Will love die without a body to contain it?
Or can the spirit of it, hover around
timeless, ageless, reckless?
What if you do get that chance
and dismiss it.
Will it ever come again?
Or is it just a fantasy
without foundation?
Part of a dream.

AND THEN I REMEMBER

I sometimes miss you
Even now.
It weighs heavy in my heart.
Making no sense to me.
You are not the person you seemed.
And I know this, I accept it.
But sometimes, not always, but sometimes.
I miss the way you made me feel.
I miss the times we shared. Our intensity.
How much we laughed and loved.
Then I remember;
Your cruel words when I came clean.
Taking away your control.
That you placed the blame on me.
That you only worried about yourself.
Then I remembered;
That you ran and called the police.
When he came to confront.
Then had him followed for days.
A coward to your own people.
I wonder if they laughed. I know we did.
Then I remembered;
That you never faced all you wronged.
You never said you were sorry.
That you feel no remorse towards me, or him.
Just about me, and only because you were caught.
I never thought I could love someone like you.
Yet, I have. I did.
It makes my heart heavy with confusion.
Sometimes I forget.
And then I remember.

MISSING SOMETHING

I miss feeling my smile in my eyes.
I miss stolen kisses and sad good byes.
I miss my heart stopping at the ring of a phone.
I miss the sensual thoughts when I am alone.
I miss drive bye waves and window views.
I miss my inspiration, my poetic muse.
I miss trusting others, and being trusted
I miss trusting myself since my judgement is busted.
I miss my lost dignity and my moral virtue
I miss having my cake and eating it too.
I miss being naive that some acquaintances were friends.
I miss wanting to help them, but my give a damn ends.
I miss feeling happy or sad, and the many tears wasted.
I miss feeling anything, and the life that I tasted.
I miss justifying my actions with emotional divorce.
I miss not owning my mistakes or not having to feel remorse.
I miss Sunday morning phone calls, and those at the gym.
I miss not needing therapy and not having to looking within.
I miss my acceptance of how things are meant to be.
Most of all, what I miss the most, is me.

NO CONTACT

I can't touch you,
hear you, Or see you.
It's no longer allowed.
But I can whisper your name.
Ears alone cannot hear it.
Said for the night sky.
Just to make the stars twinkle,
and the moon grin
At my hidden thoughts.
You may sense my whisper
in a tranquil breeze.
Caressing your neck.
Reminding you of my fingertips.
If you are watching the same sky.
The stars are waving hello for me,
bright and cheerful, again reminding.
The moon reflecting my smile.
Lighting your way in the dark.
When I feel you in the atmosphere.
Do you feel me?
I have all I need in my physical world.
There is no room for you there.
I can keep you in the realm of space.
A tryst in my cosmic imagination.
Where I can't touch you,
see you, or hear you.
But I can whisper your name.

TRIGGERS

Following,reminding, everywhere.
In two tone Fords, and mini vans too.
In classic rock songs on the radio.
Anything by Journey and some Who.
In certain stores and paint stickers.
In Styrofoam coffee cups. Even in the creamer.
In gold solitaires and silver watches.
Weirdly enough, in seeing a Beamer.
In driving by certain roads. Bittersweet.
Seeing family or even some friends.
I wish the reminders would just go away
but the feeling never ends.
When they trigger me, they set him off too.
He senses sadly what I'm thinking.
Shaking hands give me away,
He knows my stomach is sinking.
Everything comes back, it's so hard not to cry,
For days my heart is a remorseful blue.
He'll hold my hand and smile, so I focus on him.
Sometimes that is a trigger too.

I WISH FOR HIM
(The Other Guy)

I wish the best for you
That is just how I'm made.
I can't have you in my life
But I want you to be happy.
To be true to yourself.
Wouldn't it be amazing,
If you could really be the person
you pretended to be?
If you could take your ability
to read people,
and understand their needs,
 Their vulnerabilities.
And help them. For their benefit alone-
And not your own.
If you could make someone feel
special, beautiful, and valuable
and mean it with all your heart.
No expectations in return.
Because that is where the happiness is;
In giving love, not receiving .
In smiling and getting smiles.
In joking and making laughter.
In teasing to experience a fresh blush.
To touch and feel someone's energy.
It's true.
In giving love you are receiving.
I was happy loving you.
Thank you dearly for letting me.
Someday, I really pray
for you to be-
The person you pretended to be.
Not for her, not for me
But for yourself and humanity.

MY FRIEND

I could not confide in you, my friend.
Although, I know your shoulders are strong.
Its an unfair burden to ask you to carry.
To keep my secrets and cover my lies.
I chose to do it all on my own.
You would have been there for me.
I know.
Not condoning but supporting.
Because you are my friend.
You would have shared the laughter,
and dried my tears, given me strength.
Your amazing loyalty.
Please don't think I didn't trust you.
I wanted to spare your conscience.
Keep you from my wrongs.
Now, even knowing them, you are here.
My rock of sanity in my dark times.
And I Thank you.

RECONCILING

"If the foundation is good…the rest can be fixed."
—The Money Pit

LOVING ME ANYWAY

Vacant eyes in an empty shell.
He traces his finger across my cheek
My smile forms in lips only.
He watches me, deep into my eyes.
Looking for any sign I've come back.
He fears the soulless.
Whispering softly.
Asking if I'm with him.
He knows he pushed me away.
He lost me. Trying to find me again.
Wanting to know if he's on the right path.
I'm with him in body. My spirit drifting.
He refuses to let go.
Pulling me to him. Hand over hand.
I want to trust him.
That when he gets me back
he won't just push me away.
Because he can't lose me.
Never again. I am his heart
He knows this now.
When I left it stopped beating.
It died inside, only to be reborn.
With a new clarity.
So many regrets. So much guilt.
He wishes he could have protected me
from my pain.
Never again will he let me feel vulnerable.
The door to his heart is open.
Waiting for me to come home.
I am his wife, his life,
Forever.
Despite my wrongs.
He loves me anyway.

HYSTERICAL BONDING

Take me, all of me, again and again.
With neanderthal possession.
Sweat all traces of sin from my skin.
My every pore consumed
with your anger, love and confusion.
Holding my hair in your fist
brow to brow.
Daring me to look away…
as if I could.
The heat of carnal kisses
bruising my lips in punishment.
Sheathing yourself in
walls once sacred.
Pulsating your torment into me.
Claiming.
Marking your territory.
The release of fiery liquid passion,
burning into the center of my desire.
Permanently scarring. A reminder.
That you can take me like this.
In consummate bonding.
Again and again.

MY GUIDING LIGHT

In my fog of confusion
you have been my lighthouse
directing me safely home.
Weathering the stormy times.
Waves of chaos crashing
over rocky emotions
Yet you do not waver.
Holding strong.
Dependable and loyal.
My husband, my love.
You are the light.
Forever guiding.

SHATTERED SOULS

When I was shattered by another
you were there to pick up the pieces
and put me back together.
In your anger and betrayal;
You could have swept up the shards
and thrown them away.
Instead, you laid out the fragments,
considered their fragility and strengths.
You studied them, isolated, seeing your
own faults and weaknesses.
Gaining full understanding the damage
caused and your hand in it.
You chose to help me restore myself
when you had the tools to finish me off.
Proving patience you thought impossible
you caressed each chip tenderly,
placed it in your palm, and set it on another.
With care, you took another and another,
until the delicate fragments coming together
formed an image of me from memory.
If you came to a piece that didn't seem to fit,
You had the strength to find help and direction.
Never forcing them to conform.
You searched for another piece to fill the void.
At times openly giving a piece of yourself.
Intermingling, we became two people whole with
each other.
Our love the glue that holds us together.
Stronger, reinforced with a lifetime of value.

Handle us with care.

HAND TO HEART

A country stroll
holding hands
fingers interwoven
a firm grasp
of unity
for all to see.
An impenetrable force
faced with adversity.
Love worth hanging onto
in a world of letting go.
Committing hearts
by first holding hands.
On a country stroll.

HELP ME LET GO

Lay your hands on me softly,
and wipe away his touch.
Whisper to me sweetly,
Til I no longer hear his voice.
Hold my hand firmly,
and keep me by your side.
Fill my heart with love,
to squeeze out all the hate.
Ease yourself inside me,
to regain your sacred place.
Look me in the eyes,
so I can see a real man.
No other can replace.

FORGIVEN

In the twilight of slumber
Star shadows danced on the nudes.
Shallow breath blowing in my hair.
Sensations across my ear.
Circled by arms of heavy comfort.
Cupping my breasts.
Dare I dream?
Anvil of emotions exhaust me.
The days guilt draining.
I won't wake up.
I want to keep this feeling.
Safe in lost consciousness.
Dawn and twilight share a quick dance.
Sun taunting the hope of a new day.
Enveloped in a blanket of warmth.
Golden glow on naked skin.
A rough hand gently wanders.
My belly trembles with his touch.
Anticipating.
My dream is my reality.
I have awakened.
He's still here.

MONSTERS

Shadows in a dark room.
Covers thrown back,
gasping for air.
Trembling in desperation.
The monsters he fears
aren't under the bed.
They are in his head.
I brought them in our home.
The images of me with another.
Killing him slowly
through his imagination.
We will fight them together.
I'm right here beside him.
Turning on the light.
So he can see me. Only me.
His eyes focus. Taking me in.
I'm here. I kiss his brow.
Eyes close in rest.
Slumber resumed.
I watch him protectively.
Holding him close.
Keeping the light on.
Just in case.

THIS IS HEAVEN

Lying in the crook of your arm
Your heartbeat against my cheek.
The hairs on your chest softly teasing.
I inhale the scent known only to you.
Nipples tighten as I exhale
Your body aware of me as you sleep.
I find comfort in that power.
This is where I belong.
Skin to skin against you.
The morning sun warms.
Playing with our senses.
It's time to start our day.
The babies sleeping, it's only us.
Your mind follows body in arousal,
We love quietly.
The doors to our hearts have been opened
for all to see.
but not this morning.
This is our time. No one can invade.
The monsters of the night freed.
Disappearing with the morning light.
Alone together, sweetly spent.
Enjoying our heaven.

THOSE THREE WORDS

How do I tell you,
That I have such intense feelings for you
without you breaking down my protective wall?
How do I tell you   -
that Im vulnerable to your feelings and thoughts
Without giving you power to hurt me?
How do I tell you-
that you're the missing piece of my puzzle.
The complete picture.
Without you hiding the glue?
How do I tell you   -
That I have found happiness and trust and wholeness.
Without you taking advantage?
How do I tell you-
That you are my oasis in the dry desert that I've crossed.
Without letting you deny me water?
How do I tell you-
That you are all the seasons. Through sunshine and storms.
Spring is my favorite. Full of hope.
Without taking a Fall?
I guess I just say-
I trust you.
I love you.

MY KNIGHT

A man of honor
My knight in shining armor
chaser of intangible dragons
the ones I have created.
My protector
strong and loyal.
A man of truth and justice
of self reflection and ownership.
A bigger man for my mistakes.
Because you didn't let go.
So easy to give up
to let hurt and pain prevail.
Never a coward.
You don't run from dragons.
You meet them head on.
Slay them or tame them.
A knight in shining armor.

DRIVE THROUGH LIFE

On our drive through life-
We can't dwell on years of wrong turns,
On how many times we've been lost.
Constantly looking in the rearview mirror
will make wrecking inevitable.
We need to drive forward, looking forward,
to a new destination.
Yesterdays miles took us where we are today.
Today's decide where we go tomorrow.
We need to stay between the lines and
Follow the rules of the road.
Look for guidance in the signs around us,
and be open to altering our course.
Change lanes to pass those slowing us down.
While accepting the roadblocks and detours with ease.
Asking for direction if we lose our way.
We'll make this journey together.
Driving forward all the way.

STARTING OVER

We can not go back.
The old marriage a thing of the past.
We have to let go.
The resentment a poison to our future.
Reconciling does not just mean staying together.
It means a fresh beginning, an new relationship.
We survived adversity with fresh strength.
Found new love in ourselves.
A new freedom in complete honesty.
No more secrets, no more lies.
If we love we say so.
If we hate we say that too.
No hiding from our vulnerabilities.
Sharing openly.
Touching, feeling, holding without restriction.
Showing support in our wants.
Expressing desire of our needs.
Realizing that our wants and needs may
not be the same.
Respecting each others individuality.
Complimenting what makes us unique.
Appreciating all efforts big or small.
Being reasonable in our expectations.
While always striving to improve.
Making time, Making love, Making it work.
Making it together.

ON THIS DAY

The sun high in the blue.
Grass soft to bare feet.
The cheerful chaos of children playing.
So pleasant to my ears.
Sun kissed and thoughtful,
my heart drifts.
I think about him rarely.
The other man.
His importance small.
We began a year ago this day.
The end still too new to
completely let go.
He no longer has a hold on me.
Just memories.
A phantom love.
No longer there.
Like a missing part of myself.
Ever so small.
I remember the feeling
of that love.
It's not a real love to act on.
An itch I can't scratch.
The real love,
the love of my husband,
Is my main focus now.
Along with my children.
My watch ticks slowly as
I wait for him to come home.
Eager to embrace him.

A bouquet of dandelions-
picked by tiny fingers,
brings me back.
Their yellow fairy dust decorating
tan skin.
It's so easy to smile now.
I found contentment.
This is my life, where my value lies.
I will use this day as a reminder.
Not of what I don't have-
but of what I do.
Happy Anniversary.

ONE REAL MAN

One real man
and then you were two
Times the man
my heart let me see
you are the only one
and then you were three
Times the man
whom I'll always adore
as the love of my life
and then you were four
Times the man
all others should strive
to find your inner strength
and then you were five
Times the man
not out for a quick fix
hanging on through adversity
and then you were six
Times the man
one worthy of Heaven
one I'll always look up to
and then you were seven
Times the man
for stepping up to the plate
we are on the right path.
and then you were eight
Times the man
so sexy and fine
the only one I desire
and then you were nine

Times the man
for forgiving my sin
What was I thinking?
Because you are Ten
Times the man
He could ever be
and I'm so blessed
 That you love me.

My New Vows

The honesty I promise you
may overwhelm when times are hard.
But expect no less from this marriage new.
Life isn't always a Hallmark card.
I will care for you in any sickness
and be ever grateful when in good health.
I will stick by you in financial distress
and remind you of our non material wealth.
I will share your fears, your memories.
That brought us to this place.
I will fight with you without reserve
any demons that we face.
I will lift you when your feeling low.
And gently dry your hidden tears.
We have planted our seeds, now watch them grow.
Parenting together for many years.
I will take the morning light
and use it to radiate your day.
I will hope it holds you to the night
Until warmly beside you I can lay.
I will make love to you in body
as well as to you in spirit.
I will thank God for you every day
And pray that you will hear it.
You will always be my priority
even when chaos tries to reign.
Your heart will always have seniority
There is so much more love to gain.

In my eyes you will be the focus
of our life and desired reality.
Like the early bud of a snow crocus
challenged, my eyes opened for eternity.
Know this now and forever...
For I will try to tell you in every way
You are my dearest, truest, greatest love
I vow to show you everyday.

"You are my rainbow in a sky of tears."
—NJR

This poetry will take you through my story of infidelity. I became emotionally divorced in my marriage but could see no fair way out. I fell for a married man who made every effort to bring love and joy into my life. My heart and soul crossed the line and I found myself aboard a roller coaster ride of emotions. Mind and heart were in constant conflict. Everything I had started slipping away, and everything I wanted was just out of reach. In confessing, I was faced with reality. The other man proved he was not as he seemed. I meant nothing to him. My pride bruised and my heart shattered. I had no trust left. To heal, I owned my mistakes and learned to forgive. I took my life back. My husband and I reconciled through real love and complete honesty. The poems express my thoughts through this journey.

http://dontkissfrogs.tripod.com

LaVergne, TN USA
17 December 2009
167319LV00002B/51/A